THE NEW MEDITERRANEAN DIET COOKBOOK FOR BEGINNERS

THE COMPLETE GUIDE FOR WEIGHT LOSS, WITH TIPS FOR SUCCESS AND SECRETS FOR BURN FAT AND ENJOY YOUR FOOD

SANDRA RAMOS

The New Mediterranean Diet Cookbook for Beginners

SANDRA RAMOS

Copyright - 2021 - All rights reserved.

The content contained within this book may not be reproduced, duplicated or transmitted without direct written permission from the author or the publisher.

Under no circumstances will any blame or legal responsibility be held against the publisher, or author, for any damages, reparation, or monetary loss due to the information contained within this book, either directly or indirectly.

Legal Notice:

This book is copyright protected. This book is only for personal use. You cannot amend, distribute, sell, use, quote or paraphrase any part, or the content within this book, without the consent of the author or publisher.

Disclaimer Notice:

Please note the information contained within this document is for educational and entertainment purposes only. All effort has been executed to present accurate, up to date, and reliable, complete information. No warranties of any kind are declared or implied.
Readers acknowledge that the author is not engaging in the rendering of legal, financial, medical or professional advice. The content within this book has been derived from various sources. Please consult a licensed professional before attempting any techniques outlined in this book.

By reading this document, the reader agrees that under no circumstances is the author responsible for any losses, direct or indirect, which are incurred as a result of the use of information contained within this document, including, but not limited to, - errors, omissions, or inaccuracies.

Table of Contents

INTRODUCTION 1

Chapter 1: Why this type of diet is the right for you? 5

Chapter 2: Your Mindset and this diet 9

Chapter 4: Exercise 15

Chapter 5: The recipes in this book 16

SMALL MEDITERRANEAN PLATES 18

    SEA FOOD CHEESE DIP 18

    Artichokes in Garlic 19

      Mediterranean Fondue 20

      Mini Pizza Snacks 21

      Italian Dressing Recipe 22

      Pecans with Pepper 23

      Roasted Onions 24

      Pecan and Cheddar Snacks 25

      The Ultimate Greek Sauce 26

      Omelet Eggplant Dip 27

      Bites from Red Potatoes 28

      Country Potato Chips 29

      Avocado Dip 30

      Potatoes and Onions with Herbs 31

      Homestyle Mashed Potatoes 32

Seafood Mediterranean Dip 33

Butter from Almond... 34

Potato Wedges with Herbs 35

Cucumber Sauce 36

Tuna Spread... 37

Roasted Pecan Couscous.. 38

Mushrooms Filled with Tuna 39

Almonds with Honey and Rosemary 40

Mashed Potatoes and Pesto Sauce 41

Kale Chips 42

Compote from Apples 43

Bolognese Sauce.. 44

Green Beans with Lemon and Pepper 45

Red Potatoes and Asparagus in Oven... 46

Portobello Mushrooms Filled with Vegetables 47

Baked Pears 48

SOUPS 49

Black Bean Chili 49

Zucchini Potato Soup.. 50

Spinach and Sausage Soup... 51

Nutmeg, Potato and Spinach Soup.. 52

Onion Soup with Beef 53

Strawberry Soup... 54

Artichoke Soup with Oysters.. 55

Chickpea, Garlic and Spinach Soup 56

- **Chicken Stew** 57
- **Spring Soup** 58
- **Asparagus Soup** 59
- **Lentil Soup with Spinach** 60
- **Butternut Squash and Pear Soup** 61
- **Mediterranean Soup with Vegetables** 62
- **Asparagus Soup with Cheese** 63
- **Apple Soup** 64
- **Potato Soup with Bacon** 65
- **Pesto Chicken Pasta Salad** 66

INTRODUCTION

The joy that I am feeling right now cannot be explained. This is because you have chosen me and this book as a guide to a new path – the Mediterranean one. The Mediterranean diet is like no other diet in this world and this way of eating is offering many health and weight benefits.

Right after World War II, Ancel Keys, a scientist and his colleague Paul Dudley, later known as President Eisenhower's cardiac physician made a Seven Countries Study together with couple of their colleagues. They included people from United States and people from Crete – Mediterranean island. The study was testing these people of all ages and Keys implemented the Mediterranean diet in this study as well.

The 13,000 men came from Netherlands, United States, Greece, Italy, Yugoslavia and Japan and it was estimated that fruits, vegetables, grains, beans and fish are the healthiest ingredients ever. This applies even after considering the impoverishment of WWII. Interestingly this was also estimated at the start, imagine what else they discovered.

Among everything else it was discovered that Mediterranean way of food consumption can make one person lose and maintain healthy weight. Every chapter included in this book will reveal different story about this diet plan and how can you become able to change your eating patterns. Also, you will find out that Mediterranean diet plan gives extreme amount of energy and you will become motivated

Chapter 1: Why this type of diet is the right for you?

Simply because it contains healthy plant foods and it is low in animal foods. Unlike other diets, Mediterranean diet offers more seafood and fish. Seafood and fish are way better than any other meat and the benefits of them is visible after a week or two of constant consumption. Plus, Mediterranean recipes do not leave you hungry, you are full after eating for a longer period.

With constant exercise and fruits, vegetables, legumes, nuts and whole grains (everything that this diet is) you will become the best version of yourself without doubt. Also, you will learn how to perfectly switch bad ingredients with good ingredients. For example, instead of butter you will start using canola or olive oil. Instead of salt you will start using different herbs and spices. Print out the Mediterranean pyramid of foods and you won't regret it.

These recipes are family friendly and you'll be able to host and enjoy and host many gatherings with your friends as well because they are also friend friendly. Occasional glass of red wine is okay, so you are good to go.

HEALTH BENEFITS

Healthy fats are the key component when it comes to Mediterranean cuisine. Also, let's not forget about the most important thing this diet has – plant-based food. Yes, this diet does not remove many food groups, but the mixture of ingredients won't make you a single problem and you will learn what goes with what in time.

But let's elaborate on the health benefits a little bit more. It is scientifically proven that the Mediterranean diet is able to lower the risk of strokes and heart disease. Every patient that has used this diet style so far, has shown lowered levels of oxidized low-density lipoprotein or LDL cholesterol (the bad cholesterol which gets build up in your arteries and causes problems with your heart.

NO MORE HEART PROBLEMS AND STROKES

One of the main ingredients in the Mediterranean diet, extra virgin olive oil, contains alpha-linolenic acid and the Warwick Medical School delivered a study that indicated how olive oil is able to decrease blood pressure. Not only that but also the olive oil is able to lower hypertension because it keeps human arteries clearer and more dilated. Also, it makes the nitric oxide more bioavailable and you won't have problems with cholesterol levels anymore. Only if of course, you consume olive oil (extra virgin) on regular bases.

If you are feeling numbness, weakness, headaches, confusion, vision problems, dizziness or slurred speech do not worry no more. This diet helps and improves this condition together with the ultimate problem – strokes that are happening due to bleeding in the brain or blocked blood vessel.

IMPROVED VISION

Another thing that would improve after starting with this diet is your vision. This diet will help you prevent or stave off the risk of macular degeneration which happens to adults over 54. This disease brings blindness and occurs to over 10 million Americans. Imagine the benefit in here, imagine being victorious against something that is able to destroy your retina and remove the chance of clear vision. The vegetables this diet promotes, the green leafy ones have lutein and that lowers the chance of experiencing cataracts as well.

WEIGHT LOSS

You probably want to lose weight as well and the search for the perfect diet that will be able to provide you that is endless. Until now. This diet is also able to give you the chance to lose weight naturally and easily with nutrient rich foods. The focus in here is on healthy fats while carbohydrates are not that present. They are still here as pasta or bread of course, but their implementation is generally low. The healthy fats, protein and fiber will allow you to lose weight and at the same time will keep you satisfied. Thanks to these nutrients you won't have cravings for candy, chips or cookies no more. The vegetables that you'll consume will fill your stomach and you won't feel hunger for hours. You won't even experience spike in your blood sugar.

IMPROVED AGILITY

According to studies, 70 percent of the seniors who have risk of developing frailty or other muscle weakness lowered the factors of experiencing that by implementing this diet in their lives.

YOU'LL START ENJOYING NATURAL FOODS

This is probably the best thing that this diet brings because it is kind of a new characteristic that you'll develop. As previously noted, this diet is low in sugar and processed foods so its recipes will bring you closer to organic produced foods thus closer to nature. For example, this diet offers honey instead of sugar and this change is priceless.

IMPROVED ASTHMA SYMPTOMS

Another study which included children revealed that antioxidant diet is able to help them decrease their asthma symptoms and at the same time made them not like eating a food that is quite popular – red meat. Yes, this diet helps children to say no to red meat and yes to plant-based food.

NO MORE ALZHEIMER'S RISK

Those people that choose this diet plant without doubt lower their risk of getting Alzheimer's disease in the future. In fact, the latest study shows that getting Alzheimer's is reduced by 40 percent to those people that consume Mediterranean diet foods. Additional exercises are recommended in the process as well.

HELPS PEOPLE WITH DIABETES

Excessive insulin is controlled with Mediterranean diet. Not every diet is able to do this and not every diet can control blood sugar levels and control your weight at the same time. As I told before this diet is at the same time low in sugar and high in healthy acids. This makes a balance for your body and burns fat while gives you energy at the same time.

The American Heart Association reveals that this diet unlike other diets is low in saturated fat while high in fat. This keeps your hunger under control and delivers amazing weight loss results.

MEDITERRANEAN DIET HELPS YOUR BRAIN

Sugar is usually responsible for the highs and lows when it comes to your mood. This diet does not contain artificial sugar at all this your mood and overall brain health will improve as well.

THE WEIGHT LOSS JOURNEY

Planning breakfast, lunch or dinner is not hard, but the part gets tricky when it comes to snacking time. You should make something for yourself that contains from 150 to 200 calories. For example, you can choose apple, pear, grapefruit and a pinch of salt.

The path that this diet offers is the safest when it comes to losing weight. Everything is healthy here and there won't be bouncing.

But many people ask what happens when the time is stumbling on us and when we do not have time to cook the meals present in here. Well, I and this diet of course have a solution for you. Trust me you will like it.

- Fruit slices – pears and apples
- Nut butter – cashew butter, almond butter and more
- Dates and figs
- Tuna salad
- Crackers
- Greek Yogurt
- Olives
- Pitas
- Hummus

Chapter 2: Your Mindset and this diet

In order to remove the unwanted pounds, you have to set your mindset on it like never before. Do not think about that all the time, start thinking about something entirely else while you are focused on losing weight. Or in other words, keep yourself busy while you consume Mediterranean diet foods and you regularly exercise. Also do not expect quick fixes. Time is all you need and after successfully sticking to the plant you'll start to realize the change and how big it is.

To be sincere, the Mediterranean diet is the one thing that you have been missing for so long. You are already motivated I think so all you have to do is start. You already purchased this book, so you are on the right path.

Write down your reasons for starting this journey and every time you are feeling down, or you lack motivated read them out loud. Write down your goals as well. Start with something small and increase as time passes.

Another important thing that people usually forget are their surroundings. It is important for you to surround with people that are positive. Positive mindset regardless of what you do is important, especially when it comes to losing weight and changing something as diet pattern. This is how you'll become able to develop emotionally, healthy realistic goals (do not forget to set your goals first).

Focus on your sleep and develop a healthy sleeping pattern as well. Recharging and sleeping for more than 7 hours are essential when it comes to weight loss because you need extreme amount of energy and sharpness. Good energy and brain sharpness appear only when one is able to properly relax and recharge in the evening hours.

Chapter 3: Nutrition and Portions

Start being aware of the things you consume now. Develop your management skills and stick to the guidelines that this book gives. What to consume? Well start with:

- Vegetables – raw and leafy
- Fruit
- Legumes
- Grains (one slice of bread is allowed)
- Dairy
- Meat
- Potatoes
- Nuts

This is the food you must start combining and portions that include these ingredients will make you set and ready for reaching your goals.

This is a sustainable diet so you won't have serious problems, but I will be lying if I say that cravings won't appear. If you successfully understand your cravings, you'll remove them and soon be proud of your dietary success. Remember, cravings for certain foods indicate need of something entirely else, something that your body is need of.

So, the adjustments that you have to make regarding the cravings are:

- Remove salty cravings with couple of nuts or seeds because your body want silicon.

- Remove fatty and oily foods with spinach, broccoli, cheese and fish because your body wants calcium and chloride.

- Remove sugary foods with chicken, beef, lamb, liver, cheese, cauliflower and broccoli because your body wants phosphorous and tryptophan.

- Remove chocolate cravings (this is the hardest one) with spinach, nuts, seeds, broccoli and cheese because your body wants magnesium and chromium.

You also have to:

- Learn how to recognize every healthy ingredient on the labels. Take back everything that does not look good to your or that indicates that there are many artificial preservatives present.

- Check your serving size.

- Always calculate your calories intake

- Consume food rich in calcium, iron, fiber, vitamin A and vitamin C.

Do not consume:

- Added sugar or foods like candy, soda, ice cream and more.

- Refined oils – soybean oil, canola oil cottonseed oil and more.

- Trans fats – margarine, soda, processed meats, beverages, table sugar and more.

- Processed meat.

- Refined grains.

Foods that you should consume:

- Seafood and Fish: Mussels, clams, crab, prawns, oysters, shrimp, tuna, mackerel, salmon, trout, sardines, anchovies, and more

- Poultry: Turkey, duck, chicken, and more

- Eggs: Duck, quail, and chicken eggs

- Dairy Products: Contain calcium, B12, and Vitamin A: Greek yogurt, regular yogurt, cheese, plus others

- Tubers: Yams, turnips, potatoes, sweet potatoes, etc.

- Vegetables: Another excellent choice for fiber, and antioxidants: Cucumbers, carrots, Brussels sprouts, tomatoes, onions, broccoli, cauliflower, spinach, kale, eggplant, artichokes, fennel, etc.

- Seedsand Nuts: Provide minerals, vitamins, fiber, and protein: Macadamia nuts, cashews, pumpkin seeds, sunflower seeds, hazelnuts, chestnuts, Brazil nuts, walnuts, almonds, pumpkin seeds, sesame, poppy, and more

- Fruits: Excellent choices for vitamin C, antioxidants, and fiber: Peaches, bananas, apples, figs, dates, pears, oranges, strawberries, melons, grapes, etc.

- Spices and Herbs: Cinnamon, garlic, pepper, nutmeg, rosemary, sage, mint, basil, parsley, etc.

- Whole Grains: Whole grain bread and pasta, buckwheat, whole wheat, barley, corn, whole oats, rye, quinoa, bulgur, couscous 18

- Legumes: Provide vitamins, fiber, carbohydrates, and protein: Chickpeas, pulses, beans, lentils, peanuts, peas

- Healthy Fats: Avocado oil, avocados, olive oil, olive oil products and olives

- Beverages: Water and tea

- White meat: Consume them but remove the visible fat and skin

- Red meat: You can consume lamb, pork, and beef in small amounts

- Potatoes: Prepare them with caution but consume them because they are excellent source of potassium, vitamin b, vitamin c and fibers.

- Desserts and sweets: consume cakes, biscuits and sweets in extra small amounts.

There is one thing that you can implement that will make your journey even more beautiful – spices and herbs! Traditional Mediterranean diet is filled with different spices and herbs and each has a different health benefit! Believe it or not herbs and spices are able to do that and that is one of the main reasons why people implement them in their diet. Here are the spices you must include and the benefits they bring:

- Anise – improves digestion, reduces nausea and alleviates cramps.

- Bay leaf – treats migraines.

- Basil – aids digestion and reduces anxiety and stress.

- Black pepper – promotes nutrient absorption and speeds up your metabolism.

- Cayenne pepper – increases metabolism and controls your appetite.

- Sweet and spicy cloves – relive pain, gum and tooth pain. Also, kill bacteria, fungal infections and aid digestive problems.

- Fennel – improves bone health.

- Garlic – improves blood sugar levels and helps you lose weight.

- Ginger – serves as diuretic and increases urine elimination.

- Marjoram – promotes healthy digestion and fights type 2 diabetes.

- Mint – treats nasal congestion, nausea, dizziness and headaches.

- Oregano – treats common cold and reduces infections. It also relieves menstrual pain.

- Parsley – improves your skin, prostate, dental health and blood circulation.

- Rosemary – increases hair growth, reduces stress, inflammation and improves pain.

- Sage – improves your digestion problems.

- Thyme – has antibacterial properties.

Chapter 4: Exercise

Mediterranean diet is extremely flexible, and you won't have problems while being out with friends. Many recipes in the restaurants come from this particular diet so, you are good to go as long as you do not eat junk food and food that is high in sugar.

Eat slowly and chew your food better. Put your utensils down between bites because that is going to help you slow down the process of eating.

The tips above will help you a lot, but nothing will help you more in this journey than exercising. Two years ago, one scientific research that mainly focused on the Mediterranean diet revealed that this diet is extremely beneficial and gets its full potential when exercise is included. So, to keep your weight under control and to lose weight at the same time you must exercise.

Do not force yourself, start with something easy and small. Spend 30 to 60 minutes daily on that part. Walk, run, do yoga, swim, ride a bike, or simply infiltrate yourself into a regular exercise program online or in a gym near you.

Regular physical activity does not improve only your look, it also improves your strength, mood and balance.

Chapter 5: The recipes in this book

This book contains 500 recipes in total. Each recipe is designed according to the rules Mediterranean diet has. Every recipe is healthy, and every recipe should be made with the best ingredients available – the organic ones. There is also a section for vegans and vegetarians. We wanted to include every person possible in this journey because this journey is all about health and improving yourself and the way you eat. At the bottom of this book you will find a meal plan that we think is going to help you a lot in the few first months. The start won't be that hard, but it is going to be challenging I must admit.

The cooking skills

It is important to know that the Mediterranean do not require hours and hours in the kitchen. The way these recipes are prepared is easy and convenient.

SMALL MEDITERRANEAN PLATES

SEA FOOD CHEESE DIP

COOKING: 20 MIN

SERVES: 2

INGREDIENTS

- 1 (8 ounce) package processed cheese food
- 2 tablespoons reduced-fat cream cheese
- 1/2 cups sour cream
- 1/2 cup cooked small shrimp
- 1/2 cup cooked crabmeat, flaked
- 1/2 cup cooked lobster, flaked
- 1 teaspoons seafood seasoning
- 1 teaspoon Worcestershire sauce
- 1 loaf (1/2-inch-thick) slices French bread, lightly toasted

NUTRITIONAL VALUE
120 calories per serving

DIRECTIONS

Mix processed cheese food, cream cheese, sour cream, shrimp, crab, and lobster in a crockpot. Cover and cook on Low heat until cheese is melted, about 1 hour, stirring occasionally to break up lumps. Once the cheese is melted, stir in seafood seasoning and Worcestershire sauce. Serve with French bread.

SMALL MEDITERRANEAN PLATES

Artichokes in Garlic

COOKING: 20 MIN   SERVES: 2

INGREDIENTS

4 ounces small uncooked seashell pasta
2 1/2 tablespoons extra virgin olive oil
3 tablespoons butter
2 cloves garlic
1 sprig fresh basil, chopped
1 (8 ounce) can artichoke hearts, drained and quartered

NUTRITIONAL VALUE
126 calories per serving

DIRECTIONS

1. Bring a pot of lightly salted water to a boil. Add seashell pasta, cook for 8 to 10 minutes, until al dente, and drain.
2. Heat the olive oil and melt the butter in a skillet over medium heat. Mix in the garlic, basil, and artichoke hearts, and cook 5 minutes, until heated through. Toss with the cooked pasta to serve.

SMALL MEDITERRANEAN PLATES

Mediterranean Fondue

COOKING: 20 MIN

SERVES: 2

INGREDIENTS

1 lb. shelled shrimp
juice of 1 lemon
8 oz. Gruyere cheese
2 pints chicken stock
1/4 cup chopped dill
pinch cayenne pepper
1/2 tsp. pepper
1/2 tsp. Sugar
2 onions

NUTRITIONAL VALUE
126 calories per serving

DIRECTIONS

1. Sprinkle shrimp with lemon juice and leave 10 minutes. Peel and chop onions. Grate cheese. Pour stock into metal fondue and heat. Add grated cheese and stir over low heat until melted; do not boil. Remove from heat, stir in onions, dill, cayenne, sugar and pepper. Bring pan to table and place on spirit burner. Drain shrimp, pat dry. Spear on fondue forks, dip in to fondu for 1 minute, then eat. Serve with slices of crusty Italian bread, hot.

SMALL MEDITERRANEAN PLATES

Mini Pizza Snacks

COOKING: 36 MIN   SERVES: 2

INGREDIENTS

1. 2 English muffins
2. 1/2 cup spaghetti sauce
3. 1 oz. mozzarella cheese oregano

NUTRITIONAL VALUE
228 calories per serving

DIRECTIONS

1. Cut the English muffins and add sauce, cheese and oregano on it. Bake at 400 degrees for 15 minutes.

SMALL MEDITERRANEAN PLATES

Italian Dressing Recipe

COOKING: 20 MIN

SERVES: 2

INGREDIENTS

DIRECTIONS

3/4 cup wine vinegar
2/3 cup red wine
1 clove garlic
1 tsp. salt
2 tsp. capers
1/2 cup oil
1 tbsp. mustard seed
2 peppers - green or red
2 tsp. prepared mustard
1 tsp. black pepper
1 tsp. rosemary - dried
1 tsp. oregano - dried

NUTRITIONAL VALUE
200 calories per serving

1. Mix vinegar and wine set for 1 hour. Finely chop garlic. Add salt, capers, mustard seed and pound to paste. Remove pepper insides and cut into slivers. Boil garlic paste, add peppers and spices, stirring. Remove from heat, add oil, cool.

SMALL MEDITERRANEAN PLATES

Pecans with Pepper

COOKING: 20 MIN

SERVES: 2

INGREDIENTS

1 teaspoon finely ground black pepper
1 teaspoon ground white pepper
1 teaspoon ground cayenne pepper
1/2 teaspoon ground paprika
1/2 teaspoon ground dried thyme
2 egg whites
1 tablespoon Worcestershire sauce
1 teaspoon hot pepper sauce
1/8 teaspoon liquid smoke flavoring (optional)

NUTRITIONAL VALUE
600 calories per serving

DIRECTIONS

1. Preheat an oven to 375 degrees F (190 degrees C). Spray a large heavy roasting pan with cooking spray.
2. Mix black pepper, white pepper, cayenne pepper, paprika, and dried thyme in a small bowl. Set aside.
3. Whisk egg whites in a large bowl until foamy. Add Worcestershire, hot sauce, and liquid smoke flavoring and whisk to mix. Drop in pecans and stir to coat well. Pour coated pecans into a colander to drain off extra egg white mixture; return to bowl and add the pepper mixture. Stir well to coat each pecan with spices.
4. Spread pecans in prepared roasting pan. Roast in preheated oven for 5 minutes and stir pecans; roast an additional 5 minutes and stir again. Turn off heat and roast pecans an additional 5 to 10 minutes until pecans are lightly browned and fragrant. Let cool and serve at room temperature.

SMALL MEDITERRANEAN PLATES

Roasted Onions

COOKING: 20 MIN

SERVES: 2

INGREDIENTS

DIRECTIONS

4 medium unpeeled yellow onions
2 tablespoons olive oil
Salt and fresh ground pepper
Balsamic vinegar (optional)

NUTRITIONAL VALUE
136 calories per serving

1. Adjust oven rack to lowest position; heat to 425 degrees.
2. Cut onions in half; toss with oil and a generous sprinkle of salt and pepper. Place cut side down, on a lipped cookie sheet.
3. Roast until tender and cut surfaces are golden brown, 25 to 30 minutes. Adjust seasonings, drizzle with balsamic vinegar.

SMALL MEDITERRANEAN PLATES

Pecan and Cheddar Snacks

COOKING: 20 MIN   SERVES: 2

INGREDIENTS

1/2 cup all-purpose flour
1 tablespoon biscuit baking mix
1 pinch cayenne pepper
1/4 cup butter or margarine, softened
1/2 cup shredded Cheddar cheese
1 egg, beaten
1 cup crisp rice cereal
1/2 cup chopped pecans

NUTRITIONAL VALUE
369 calories per serving

DIRECTIONS

1. In a bowl, combine the flour, biscuit mix and cayenne. Stir in butter until crumbly. Add cheese and egg; mix well. Stir in cereal and nuts. Shape into 1-1/2 in. balls; place on an ungreased baking sheet.
2. Bake at 350 degrees F for 18-20 minutes or until lightly browned. Serve warm.

SMALL MEDITERRANEAN PLATES

The Ultimate Greek Sauce

COOKING: 20 MIN

SERVES: 2

INGREDIENTS

1-pound ground beef
3 small onions, chopped
1 (8 ounce) can tomato sauce
1 cup water
1/2 teaspoon salt
1/2 teaspoon ground black pepper
Dried Oregano
1/2 teaspoon dried basil
1/2 teaspoon garlic powder
1/2 teaspoon ground cumin
1 teaspoon crushed red pepper flakes
2 teaspoons prepared yellow mustard

NUTRITIONAL VALUE
258 calories per serving

DIRECTIONS

1. Place the beef in a large skillet over medium heat. Cook until beef is completely brown; drain. Stir the onions, tomato sauce, water, salt, pepper, oregano, basil, garlic powder, cumin, red pepper flakes, and yellow mustard into the beef. Bring to a boil; lower heat to medium-low and simmer 45 minutes, stirring occasionally.

SMALL MEDITERRANEAN PLATES

Omelet Eggplant Dip

COOKING: 20 MIN   SERVES: 2

INGREDIENTS

1 large eggplant
3 tablespoons olive oil
1 large tomato, diced
2 cloves garlic, peeled and minced
3 eggs
salt and pepper to taste

NUTRITIONAL VALUE
246 calories per serving

DIRECTIONS

1. Preheat oven to 400 degrees F (200 degrees C).
2. Wrap eggplant in foil, and bake 35 minutes, or until soft. Remove from heat, and cool slightly. Skin and chop.
3. Heat olive oil in a medium skillet over medium heat. Stir in the tomatoes and garlic and cook until tender.
4. Mix eggplant into the skillet, and mash together with the tomato and garlic. Stir in the eggs and cook until no longer runny. Season with salt and pepper.

SMALL MEDITERRANEAN PLATES

Bites from Red Potatoes

COOKING: 20 MIN

SERVES: 2

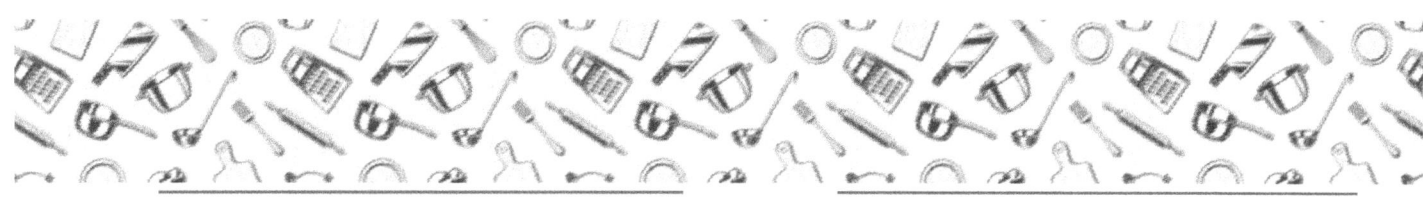

INGREDIENTS

1 1/2 pounds small round red potatoes
4 slices bacon
1 cup sour cream
1/2 teaspoon seasoned salt
1/4 teaspoon black pepper
1 tablespoon chopped fresh chives
1/2 cup shredded Cheddar cheese
Parsley

NUTRITIONAL VALUE
269 calories per serving

DIRECTIONS

1. Preheat the oven to 375 degrees F (190 degrees C). Place potatoes in a saucepan and add enough water to cover. Bring to boil, and cook until tender but still firm, about 10 minutes. Drain, and cool in a bowl of cold water.
2. Cook bacon in a skillet over medium-high heat until evenly browned. Drain, crumble, and set aside.
3. Remove cooled potatoes from water. Pat dry with a paper towel and slice in half. Using a small spoon, carefully remove a small amount from center, leaving approximately 1/4-inch rim around each potato. Set reserved potato aside.
4. In a bowl, mix together reserved potato, sour cream, bacon, seasoned salt, pepper, and chives. Spoon a small amount of mixture into each potato half and place on a baking sheet. Top each potato off with some shredded cheese.
5. Bake for 10 minutes in the preheated oven, or until cheese is melted and potatoes are warmed through. Garnish with parsley and serve.

SMALL MEDITERRANEAN PLATES

Country Potato Chips

COOKING: 20 MIN

SERVES: 2

INGREDIENTS

4 medium potatoes, peeled and sliced paper-thin
3 tablespoons salt
1-quart oil for deep frying

NUTRITIONAL VALUE
450 calories per serving

DIRECTIONS

1. Place potato slices into a large bowl of cold water as you slice. Drain, and rinse, then refill the bowl with water, and add the salt. Let the potatoes soak in the salty water for at least 30 minutes. Drain, then rinse and drain again.
2. Heat oil in a deep fryer to 365 degrees F (185 degrees C). Fry potato slices in small batches. Once they start turning golden, remove and drain on paper towels. Continue until all of the slices are fried. Season with additional salt if desired.

SMALL MEDITERRANEAN PLATES

Avocado Dip

COOKING: 20 MIN

SERVES: 2

INGREDIENTS

1 avocado - peeled, pitted and diced
clove garlic, minced
tablespoons lime juice
1 roma (plum) tomato, seeded and diced
1/4 cup crumbled feta cheese

NUTRITIONAL VALUE
365 calories per serving

DIRECTIONS

1. Mash together the avocado, garlic, and lime juice in a bowl until nearly smooth. Fold in the diced tomato and feta cheese.

SMALL MEDITERRANEAN PLATES

Potatoes and Onions with Herbs

COOKING: 20 MIN

SERVES: 2

INGREDIENTS

3 medium red potatoes, thinly sliced
medium onion, thinly sliced
1/2 teaspoon Italian seasoning
1/8 teaspoon pepper
2 tablespoons reduced-fat olive oil, melted

NUTRITIONAL VALUE
411 calories per serving

DIRECTIONS

1. In an ungreased 2-qt. microwave-safe baking dish, layer half the potato and onion slices. Mix Italian seasoning and pepper, sprinkle half over the onion and potato layer. Drizzle with 1 tablespoon olive oil. Repeat layers. Cover with vented plastic wrap. Microwave on high for 12 minutes or until potatoes are tender turning dish after 6 minutes.

SMALL MEDITERRANEAN PLATES

Homestyle Mashed Potatoes

COOKING: MIN

SERVES:

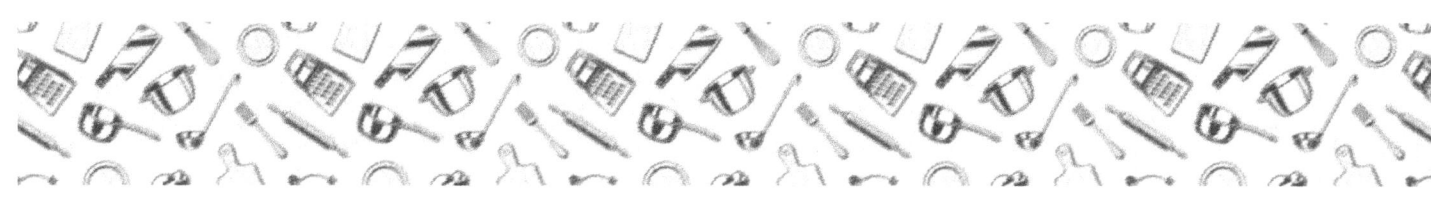

INGREDIENTS

5 medium baking potatoes, peeled and sliced
1 cup shredded Monterey Jack cheese
1/2 cup garlic seasoned breadcrumbs
1/2 cup milk
1 tablespoon butter
salt and pepper to taste

NUTRITIONAL VALUE
246 calories per serving

DIRECTIONS

1. Preheat the oven to 400 degrees F (200 degrees C).
2. Place the potatoes into a saucepan and fill with enough water to cover. Bring to a boil. Cook for 5 to 10 minutes, just until soft. Drain water, and mash potatoes. Beat in the butter, and about half of the milk using an electric mixer. Add more milk if needed to achieve the desired consistency of mashed potato. Season with salt and pepper.
3. Spread potatoes evenly in a 9x13 inch baking dish, or desired casserole dish. Sprinkle the breadcrumbs and cheese over the top.
4. Bake for about 10 minutes in the preheated oven, until the cheese is melted, and the top is browned. Serve immediately.

SMALL MEDITERRANEAN PLATES

Seafood Mediterranean Dip

COOKING: 20 MIN	SERVES: 2

INGREDIENTS

1 1/2 cups sour cream
1 cup mayonnaise
1 tablespoon dry vegetable soup mix
1 cup imitation crabmeat, diced

NUTRITIONAL VALUE
244 calories per serving

DIRECTIONS

1. In a medium-size mixing bowl, mix together sour cream, mayonnaise, vegetable soup mix, and crab. Cover and refrigerate at least one hour. Delicious!

SMALL MEDITERRANEAN PLATES

Butter from Almond

COOKING: 20 MIN

SERVES: 2

INGREDIENTS

DIRECTIONS

1 cup toasted almonds
2 teaspoons olive oil

NUTRITIONAL VALUE
400 calories per serving

1. Place the almonds in a food processor. Process on high until ground almonds begin to form a ball. Drizzle olive oil over almonds and continue to process, stopping occasionally to scrape sides of the bowl with a spatula as needed. Store in an airtight container.

SMALL MEDITERRANEAN PLATES

Potato Wedges with Herbs

COOKING: 20 MIN

SERVES: 2

INGREDIENTS

5 large potatoes, peeled and slice into wedges
1/4 cup olive oil
1/4 cup chopped fresh parsley
1 tablespoon chopped fresh thyme
1 tablespoon chopped fresh oregano
1 teaspoon salt
1 teaspoon black pepper

NUTRITIONAL VALUE
321 calories per serving

DIRECTIONS

1. Preheat oven to 450 degrees F (230 degrees C).

2. In a large bowl, toss potato wedges with oil. Arrange in a single layer in a roasting pan.

3. Bake in preheated oven for 50 minutes. Sprinkle with parsley, thyme, oregano, salt and pepper. Bake for 10 minutes, or until golden brown.

SMALL MEDITERRANEAN PLATES

Cucumber Sauce

COOKING: 20 MIN

SERVES: 2

INGREDIENTS

1 cup plain yogurt
1 cup sour cream
1 teaspoon white vinegar
1/2 teaspoon lemon juice
1 small cucumber – peeled, seeded, and finely chopped 1 green onion
1 garlic clove, minced
1/4 cup crumbled feta cheese
1/2 teaspoon oregano
1/4 teaspoon lemon zest salt and pepper to taste

NUTRITIONAL VALUE
258 calories per serving

DIRECTIONS

1. Stir together the yogurt, sour cream, vinegar, lemon juice, cucumber, green onion, garlic, feta cheese, oregano, lemon zest, salt, and pepper in a bowl; cover and chill 8 hours or overnight before serving.

SMALL MEDITERRANEAN PLATES

Tuna Spread

COOKING: 20 MIN

SERVES: 2

INGREDIENTS

1 (8 ounce) package cream cheese, softened
3 tablespoons salsa
2 teaspoons dried parsley flakes 1 teaspoon dried minced onion
1 (6 ounce) can tuna, drained and flaked

NUTRITIONAL VALUE
126 calories per serving

DIRECTIONS

1. In a bowl, mix cream cheese and salsa; stir in parsley and onion. Fold in tuna. Refrigerate until serving. Serve on bread, snack rye or crackers.

SMALL MEDITERRANEAN PLATES

Roasted Pecan Couscous

COOKING: 20 MIN   SERVES: 2

INGREDIENTS

2/3 cup pecan pieces
1 tablespoon butter
1 1/2 cups quartered fresh button mushrooms
1 onion, chopped
1 tablespoon minced fresh garlic
2 teaspoons butter
1 1/4 cups water
1 (5.8 ounce) box couscous
1 (8.5 ounce) bottle sun-dried tomato pesto
1/3 cup finely grated Parmesan cheese, or more to taste
salt and ground black pepper to taste

NUTRITIONAL VALUE
410 calories per serving

DIRECTIONS

1. Spread the pecan pieces onto a baking sheet and place in a cold oven.
2. Heat the oven to 350 degrees F (175 degrees C) to begin roasting the pecans. Roast until aromatic, 20 to 30 minutes.
3. Melt 1 tablespoon butter in a large skillet over medium heat. Cook the mushrooms, onion, and garlic in the melted butter until softened, 5 to 7 minutes. Transfer to a bowl and set aside.
4. Return the skillet to the heat. Melt 2 teaspoons butter in the skillet. Stir the water into the butter; bring to a boil. Put the couscous in a glass bowl; pour the butter and water mixture over the couscous. Immediately cover the bowl with plastic wrap and allow to sit until the couscous absorbs all of the moisture, 7 to 10 minutes. Fluff with a fork. Stir the toasted pecans, the mushroom mixture, the pesto, and Parmesan cheese through the couscous. Season with salt and pepper to serve.

SMALL MEDITERRANEAN PLATES

Mushrooms Filled with Tuna

COOKING: 20 MIN

SERVES: 2

INGREDIENTS

(6 ounce) can albacore tuna in water, drained and flaked
tablespoons mayonnaise
1/4 teaspoon dried minced onion
1/4 teaspoon onion powder
1/2 teaspoons sweet pickle relish
(1 ounce) slices Swiss cheese, diced
salt and pepper to taste
1 (8 ounce) package fresh white mushrooms, cleaned and stems removed

NUTRITIONAL VALUE
471 calories per serving

DIRECTIONS

1. Preheat an oven to 350 degrees F (175 degrees C).
2. Mix the tuna, mayonnaise, dried onion, onion powder, sweet relish, Swiss cheese, salt, and pepper in a large bowl. Fill mushroom caps with the tuna mixture; place on baking sheet.
3. Bake in preheated oven until the mushrooms are soft, and begin to give up their juices, 20 to 25 minutes.

SMALL MEDITERRANEAN PLATES

 **Almonds with Honey and Rosemary**

COOKING: 20 MIN SERVES: 6

INGREDIENTS

1 cup almonds
1 tablespoon rosemary
Salt
1 tablespoon honey

NUTRITIONAL VALUE
149 calories per serving

DIRECTIONS

1. Use the medium heat setting to warm a skillet. Toss in the rosemary, salt, and almonds.
2. Drizzle with the honey and continue cooking for 3 to 4 minutes.
3. Stir often until the almonds are well coated and starting to darken around the edges
4. Transfer to the countertop. Use a spatula to spread the almonds evenly onto a pan coated with a spritz of nonstick cooking oil spray.
5. Cool for 10 minutes and break the almonds apart right before serving.

SMALL MEDITERRANEAN PLATES

 **Mashed Potatoes and Pesto Sauce**

COOKING: 20 MIN   SERVES: 2

INGREDIENTS

8 red potatoes, peeled and cubed
2 cloves garlic, minced
1 tablespoon olive oil
1 (14 ounce) can vegetable broth
3/4 (10 ounce) bag washed fresh spinach
1/2 cup grated Parmesan cheese
Salt
Pepper

NUTRITIONAL VALUE
321 calories per serving

DIRECTIONS

1. Place potatoes into a large pot and cover with salted water. Bring to a boil over high heat, then reduce heat to medium-low, cover, and simmer until tender, about 20 minutes. Drain and allow to steam for a few minutes. Meanwhile, place garlic, olive oil, vegetable broth, and spinach into a blender. Puree until smooth and set aside.
2. When the potatoes are ready, mash until smooth, then fold in Parmesan cheese, and season to taste with salt and pepper.

SMALL MEDITERRANEAN PLATES

Kale Chips

COOKING: 20 MIN

SERVES: 4

INGREDIENTS

DIRECTIONS

1 tablespoon olive oil
5 tablespoons chili powder
Sea salt
2-inch pieces steamed kale

NUTRITIONAL VALUE
56 calories per serving

1. Warm up the oven to reach 300° Fahrenheit.
2. Line each of the pans with parchment paper.
3. Rinse and dry the kale. Add to a bowl with the olive oil.
4. Spread the kale out on the baking sheets (single layered). Roast for 25 minutes.
5. Let them cool for 5 minutes before serving.

SMALL MEDITERRANEAN PLATES

Compote from Apples

COOKING: 20 MIN

SERVES: 2

INGREDIENTS

1-pound raw honey
20 to 30 apples
2 lemons

NUTRITIONAL VALUE
301 calories per serving

DIRECTIONS

1. Take large ripe pippin apples. Pare, core, and weigh them, and to each pound allow a pound of fine raw honey and two lemons.
2. Parboil the apples, and then set them out to cool. Pare off very nicely with a penknife the yellow rind of the lemons, taking care not to break it; and then with scissors trim the edges to an even width all along.
3. Put the lemon-rind to boil in a little saucepan by itself, till it Becomes tender, and then set it to cool.
4. Allow half a pint of water to each pound of the honey; and when it is melted, set it on the fire in the preserving kettle, put in the apples, and boil them slowly till they are clear and tender all through, but not till they break; skimming the syrup carefully.
5. After you have taken out the apples, add the lemon-juice, put in the lemon-peel, and boil it till quite transparent.
6. When the whole is cold, put the apples with the syrup into glass dishes, and dispose the wreaths of lemon-peel fancifully about them.

SMALL MEDITERRANEAN PLATES

Bolognese Sauce

COOKING: 20 MIN　　　　　　　　　　　　　　　　　　　　SERVES: 2

INGREDIENTS

2 tablespoons olive oil
4 slices bacon, slice into 1/2-inch pieces
1 large onion, minced
1 clove garlic, minced
pound lean ground beef
1/2-pound ground pork
1/2-pound fresh mushrooms, sliced
carrots, shredded
1 stalk celery, chopped
1 (28 ounce) can Italian plum tomatoes
6 ounces tomato sauce
1/2 cup dry white wine
1/2 cup chicken stock
1/2 teaspoon dried basil
1/2 teaspoon dried oregano salt and pepper to taste
1-pound pasta

NUTRITIONAL VALUE
126 calories per serving

DIRECTIONS

1. In a large skillet, warm oil over medium heat and saute bacon, onion and garlic until bacon is browned and crisp; set aside.
2. In large saucepan, brown beef and pork. Drain off excess fat. Stir in bacon mixture, mushrooms, carrots, celery, tomatoes, tomato sauce, wine, stock, basil, oregano, salt and pepper to saucepan.
3. Cover, reduce heat and simmer one hour, stirring occasionally.
4. Bring a large pot of lightly salted water to a boil. Add pasta and cook for 8 to 10 minutes or until al dente; drain.
5. Serve sauce over hot pasta.

SMALL MEDITERRANEAN PLATES

 **Green Beans with Lemon and Pepper**

COOKING: 20 MIN   SERVES: 2

INGREDIENTS

- 1-pound fresh green beans, rinsed and trimmed
- 2 tablespoons butter
- 1/4 cup sliced almonds
- 2 teaspoons lemon pepper

NUTRITIONAL VALUE
301 calories per serving

DIRECTIONS

1. Place green beans in a steamer over 1 inch of boiling water. Cover, and cook until tender but still firm, about 10 minutes; drain.
2. Meanwhile, melt butter in a skillet over medium heat. Sauté almonds until lightly browned. Season with lemon pepper. Stir in green beans and toss to coat.

SMALL MEDITERRANEAN PLATES

Red Potatoes and Asparagus in Oven

COOKING: 20 MIN

SERVES: 2

INGREDIENTS

1/2 pounds red potatoes, slice into chunks
tablespoons extra virgin olive oil
8 cloves garlic, thinly sliced
4 teaspoons dried rosemary
4 teaspoons dried thyme
2 teaspoons kosher salt
1 bunch fresh asparagus, trimmed and slice into 1-inch pieces

NUTRITIONAL VALUE
126 calories per serving

DIRECTIONS

1. Preheat oven to 425 degrees F (220 degrees C).
2. In a large baking dish, toss the red potatoes with 1/2 the olive oil, garlic, rosemary, thyme, and 1/2 the kosher salt. Cover with aluminum foil.
3. Bake 20 minutes in the preheated oven. Mix in the asparagus, remaining olive oil, and remaining salt. Cover, and continue cooking 15 minutes, or until the potatoes are tender. Increase oven temperature to 450 degrees F
4. (230 degrees C). Remove foil, and continue cooking 5 to 10 minutes, until potatoes are lightly browned. Season with pepper to serve.

SMALL MEDITERRANEAN PLATES

   **Portobello Mushrooms Filled with Vegetables**

COOKING: 20 MIN   SERVES: 2

INGREDIENTS

1 cup balsamic vinegar
1/2 teaspoon garlic powder
1/2 teaspoon onion powder
4 large portobello mushrooms, wiped clean and stems removed 2 tablespoons olive oil
1 small eggplant, peeled and diced
1 cup frozen spinach
1/2 cup shredded mozzarella cheese
2 plum tomatoes, diced
1 (6 ounce) jar artichoke hearts in brine, drained and chopped
1/4 cup grated Parmesan cheese

NUTRITIONAL VALUE
126 calories per serving

DIRECTIONS

1. Stir the balsamic vinegar, garlic powder, and onion powder together in a small bowl until blended. Place the mushrooms into a large resealable plastic bag. Pour in the balsamic vinegar mixture, seal bag, and turn gently to coat mushrooms evenly with marinade.
2. Place in refrigerator for 1 hour.
3. Place the olive oil into a skillet, and heat over medium-high heat. Stir in the eggplant and spinach; cook and stir until eggplant turns golden brown, about 5 minutes.
4. Preheat oven to 350 degrees F (175 degrees C). Lightly grease 9x13 inch baking dish.
5. Remove mushrooms from marinade, shake off any excess, and discard marinade. Place mushrooms in prepared dish, top side down. Spoon the eggplant and spinach mixture evenly over the mushrooms. Sprinkle with mozzarella cheese. Divide the tomatoes and artichoke hearts evenly between the mushrooms. Top each mushroom with Parmesan cheese.
6. Place in preheated oven, and bake until the cheese melts, about 12 minutes. Serve hot.

SMALL MEDITERRANEAN PLATES

Baked Pears

COOKING: 20 MIN

SERVES: 2

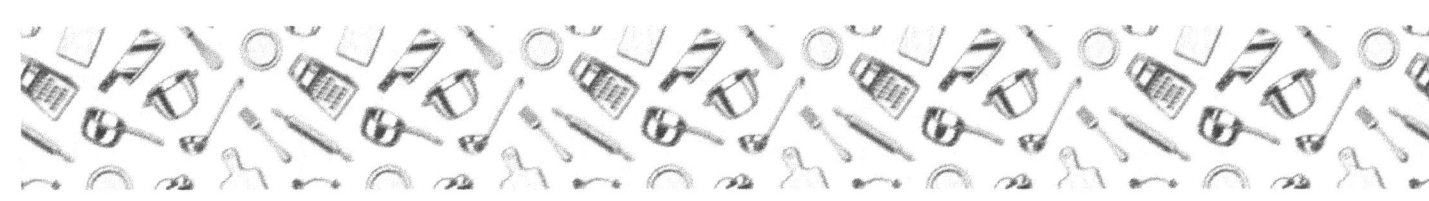

INGREDIENTS

4 pears
1 cup maple syrup
1 tablespoon cinnamon
1 teaspoon vanilla extract
Greek yogurt

NUTRITIONAL VALUE
103 calories per serving

DIRECTIONS

1. Warm up the oven to reach 375° Fahrenheit.
2. Slice each of the pears into halves. Slice off a small sliver on the underneath side so it will lay flat.
3. Remove the seeds from the core and place on a baking sheet with the face side up and sprinkle with the cinnamon.
4. Whisk the syrup and vanilla. Drizzle over the pears. Save 2 tablespoons for the garnishing.
5. Place in the oven and bake for 25 minutes or until softened.
6. When done, place in the serving dishes and drizzle with the rest of the maple syrup mixture.
7. Serve with a dollop of yogurt.

SOUPS

Black Bean Chili

COOKING: 50 MIN

SERVES: 2

INGREDIENTS

- 1/2 cup applesauce
- 1 tablespoon brown raw honey
- 1 tablespoon ground coriander
- 1 teaspoon ground cayenne pepper
- 1 teaspoon ground cumin
- 1 teaspoon dried oregano
- 1/2 teaspoon ground cloves
- 1/2 teaspoon dried rosemary
- 1/2 teaspoon dried sage
- 1/4 teaspoon dried thyme
- 1 pinch asafoetida powder (optional)
- 1 (15 ounce) can black beans
- 1 (6 ounce) can tomato paste
- 2 cloves garlic, minced
- 1 onion, chopped
- 1 yellow squash, chopped
- 2 carrots, chopped
- 1 sweet potato, peeled and diced
- 1 cup chopped fresh mushrooms
- 1-quart water, or as needed

   Nutritional Value: 223 calories per serving

DIRECTIONS

1. In a large pot over medium-low heat, mix the applesauce, brown raw honey, coriander, cayenne pepper, cumin, oregano, cloves, rosemary, sage, thyme and asafoetida powder. Cook just until heated through. Stir in black beans and tomato paste. Mix in garlic, onion, squash, carrots, sweet potato and mushrooms. Pour in enough water to cover. Bring to a boil, reduce heat to low and simmer 45 minutes, stirring occasionally.

SOUPS

Zucchini Potato Soup

COOKING: 50 MIN   SERVES: 2

INGREDIENTS

- 5 cups chicken broth
- 4 small zucchinis, thinly sliced
- 1 large potato, peeled, halved and thinly sliced
- 1 large onion, thinly sliced
- 3 eggs
- 3 tablespoons lemon juice
- 2 teaspoons dried dill weed salt and pepper to taste

Nutritional Value: 410 calories per serving

DIRECTIONS

1. In a saucepan, bring broth to a boil. Stir in zucchini, potato and onion. Reduce heat and simmer, covered, 15 minutes or until vegetables are tender. In a small bowl, beat eggs; blend in lemon juice and 1/2 cup hot broth. Stir back into the saucepan. Heat over medium for 1 minute, stirring constantly. Do not boil. Stir in dill, season with salt and pepper. Serve immediately.

SOUPS

Spinach and Sausage Soup

COOKING: 50 MIN   SERVES: 2

INGREDIENTS

DIRECTIONS

5 cups chicken broth
4 small zucchinis, thinly sliced
1 large potato, peeled, halved and thinly sliced
1 large onion, thinly sliced
3 eggs
3 tablespoons lemon juice
2 teaspoons dried dill weed salt and pepper to taste

Nutritional Value: 326 calories per serving

1. In a saucepan, bring broth to a boil. Stir in zucchini, potato and onion. Reduce heat and simmer, covered, 15 minutes or until vegetables are tender. In a small bowl, beat eggs; blend in lemon juice and 1/2 cup hot broth. Stir back into the saucepan. Heat over medium for 1 minute, stirring constantly. Do not boil. Stir in dill, season with salt and pepper. Serve immediately.

SOUPS

Nutmeg, Potato and Spinach Soup

COOKING: 50 MIN

SERVES: 2

INGREDIENTS

1 tablespoon vegetable oil
1 onion, chopped
1 1/2 quarts water
1 cube chicken bouillon
2 cups fresh spinach
4 small potatoes, peeled and halved
ground nutmeg to taste
1/2 cup milk
salt and pepper to taste

Nutritional Value: 258 calories per serving

DIRECTIONS

1. Heat the oil in a skillet over medium heat. Cook and stir the onion until tender.
2. In a saucepan, bring the water to a boil. Reduce heat to low and dissolve the bouillon cube in the water.
3. In a blender or food processor, blend the onion, spinach, potatoes, nutmeg, and about 2 cups of the bouillon until thick and smooth.
4. Blend the potato mixture into the saucepan with the remaining bouillon. Bring to a boil, reduce heat, and simmer 20 minutes. Stir in the milk and continue cooking 10 minutes. Season with salt, pepper, and more nutmeg to taste. Thus, the soup is complete.

SOUPS

 **Onion Soup with Beef**

COOKING: 50 MIN   SERVES: 2

INGREDIENTS

1 (10.5 ounce) can condensed French onion soup
1 cup cubed cooked beef
2 (3/4-inch-thick) slices French bread, toasted
1/3 cup shredded Monterey Jack cheese
2 teaspoons shredded Parmesan cheese (optional)

Nutritional Value: 201 calories per serving

DIRECTIONS

1. Prepare soup according to package Instructions; add beef. Ladle into two 2-cup ovenproof bowls. Top each with a French bread slice.
2. Sprinkle with Monterey Jack cheese and Parmesan cheese if desired. Broil until cheese is melted. Serve immediately.

SOUPS

Strawberry Soup

COOKING: 50 MIN

SERVES: 2

INGREDIENTS

DIRECTIONS

2 pints strawberries
2 cups plain yogurt
1/2 cup orange juice
1/2 cup raw honey
1/2 cup water
1/8 teaspoon ground cardamom

Nutritional Value: 369 calories per serving

1. In a blender, combine the strawberries, yogurt, orange juice, raw honey, water and cardamom. Puree until well mixed. Chill and serve.

SOUPS

Artichoke Soup with Oysters

COOKING: 50 MIN

SERVES: 2

INGREDIENTS

1 cup butter
1/2 cup chopped onion
1/2 cup chopped celery 1 cup chicken stock
1 (8 ounce) can quartered artichoke hearts, drained
1 quart fresh oysters, shucked and chopped
3 cups heavy cream
1 cup half-and-half cream

Nutritional Value: 257 calories per serving

DIRECTIONS

1. Melt butter in a large saucepan over medium heat. Saute onion and celery until tender, about 10 minutes. Pour in the chicken stock and reduce heat to low. Cook for about 15 minutes. Add the artichokes and oysters, and simmer for 10 more minutes. Finally, stir in the heavy cream and half-and-half cream. Cook until heated through, but do not boil, about 15 minutes. Serve immediately.

SOUPS

 **Chickpea, Garlic and Spinach Soup**

COOKING: 50 MIN　　　　　　　　　　　　　　　　　　　SERVES: 2

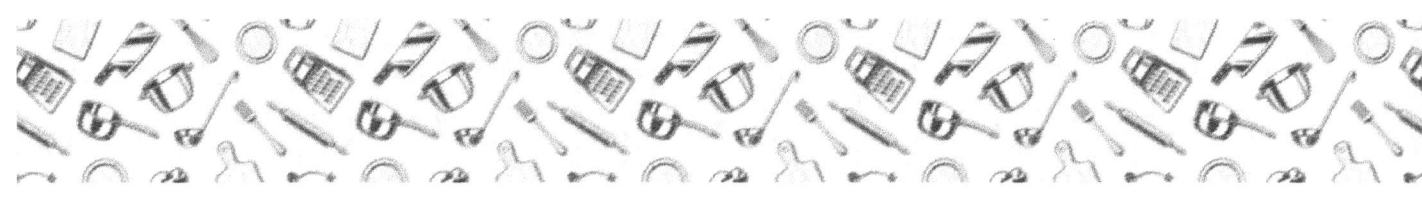

INGREDIENTS

2 tablespoons olive oil
4 cloves garlic, peeled and crushed
1 medium onion, coarsely chopped
2 teaspoons ground cumin
2 teaspoons ground coriander
1 1/3 quarts vegetable stock
3 medium potatoes, peeled and chopped
1 (15 ounce) can garbanzo beans, drained
1 cup heavy cream
2 tablespoons tahini
2 tablespoons corn meal
1/2-pound spinach, rinsed and chopped
ground cayenne pepper to taste
salt to taste

Nutritional Value: 356 calories per serving

DIRECTIONS

1. Heat olive oil in a large pot over medium heat and stir in garlic and onion. Cook until tender. Season with cumin and coriander.
2. Mix vegetable stock and potatoes into the pot and bring to a boil. Reduce heat, and simmer about 10 minutes. Stir in the garbanzo beans and continue to cook until potatoes are tender.
3. In a small bowl, blend the heavy cream, tahini, and corn meal. Mix into the soup.
4. Stir spinach into the soup. Season with cayenne pepper and salt. Continue to cook until spinach is heated through.

SOUPS

Chicken Stew

COOKING: 50 MIN

SERVES: 2

INGREDIENTS

1 cup chopped fresh parsley
8 ounces spinach, rinsed and chopped
1 onion, chopped
1 potato, cubed
4 skinless, boneless chicken breasts
6 tablespoons olive oil
1/4 teaspoon salt
1/4 teaspoon ground turmeric
2 tablespoons tomato paste
1 cup water
3 tablespoons fresh lemon juice

Nutritional Value: 547 calories per serving

DIRECTIONS

1. In a medium size frying pan, heat 4 tablespoons of the olive oil. Add the parsley and spinach and fry until wilted. Set aside.
2. Heat the other 2 tablespoons of olive oil in a large pot. Add the onion and saute, stirring occasionally, until tender. Add the chicken breasts and brown both sides of each breast. Add the salt, turmeric, fried parsley/spinach, water and tomato paste. Bring all to a boil and let boil for 10 minutes.
3. Add the cubed potatoes. Cover and let cook over low heat for 1 to 2 hours. Add the lemon juice, bring to a boil and let boil for 10 more minutes. Serve with steamed rice if desired.

SOUPS

Spring Soup

COOKING: 50 MIN SERVES: 2

INGREDIENTS

- 2 quarts beef broth
- 1 tablespoon olive oil
- 2 cups minced green onions
- 5 ounces pancetta, minced
- 1/2-pound ground veal
- 2 cups frozen artichoke hearts, thawed
- 2 cups peas
- 2 cups shelled fava beans
- 2 cups sliced fresh asparagus
- 1 1/2 teaspoons salt
- 8 slices day-old crusty bread, cut into 1-inch cubes
- 7 sprigs fresh thyme, leaves stripped
- 2 cloves garlic, crushed
- 1/2 cup olive oil
- 1/2 teaspoon salt
- ground black pepper to taste
- 13 sprigs fresh thyme, leaves stripped
- 1/2 cup grated Parmesan cheese
- 1/4 cup extra-virgin olive oil

Nutritional Value: 401 calories per serving

DIRECTIONS

1. Preheat an oven to 425 degrees F (220 degrees C). Bring beef broth to a boil in a saucepan over medium-high heat, then reduce heat to medium-low and keep hot.
2. Heat 1 tablespoon olive oil in a large pot over medium heat. Cook and stir the green onion until tender and stir in the pancetta. Cook and stir until the pancetta is browned, then increase heat to medium-high heat and stir in the ground veal. Cook and stir until the veal is crumbly, evenly browned, and no longer pink. Drain and discard any excess grease. Stir in the artichoke hearts and cook for 1 minute. Stir in the peas, fava beans, and asparagus. Season with 1 1/2 teaspoons salt. Pour in the hot beef broth and allow soup to simmer until the vegetables are tender and cooked through, 7 to 10 minutes.
3. Meanwhile, toss the slices of bread with leaves from 7 sprigs of thyme, garlic, 1/2 cup olive oil, 1/2 teaspoon salt, and pepper. Place bread on a baking sheet.
4. Toast in the preheated oven until golden brown, about 10 minutes. Set aside.
5. Stir the leaves of 13 sprigs of thyme into the soup, and season with pepper. Serve hot soup in bowls topped with croutons, Parmesan cheese, and a drizzle of extra-virgin olive oil.

SOUPS

Asparagus Soup

COOKING: 50 MIN

SERVES: 2

INGREDIENTS

1 onion, chopped
2 tablespoons butter
1-pound fresh asparagus, trimmed and coarsely chopped
1 cup vegetable broth
1 dash garlic powder
1 dash white pepper 1 cup 1% milk

Nutritional Value: 325 calories per serving

DIRECTIONS

1. Microwave onion and butter on HIGH for 2 minutes. Add asparagus, vegetable broth, garlic powder and white pepper. Microwave, covered, on HIGH for 10 to 12 minutes. Puree in blender.

2. Return mixture to microwave safe dish, stir in milk and microwave until heated through.

SOUPS

Lentil Soup with Spinach

COOKING: 50 MIN   SERVES: 2

INGREDIENTS

1 cup shredded carrots
1 large onion, chopped 1 tablespoon olive oil
6 cups water
1 (16 ounce) jar salsa
1 1/4 cups dried lentils, rinsed
3/4 teaspoon salt
1 (10 ounce) package fresh spinach, torn

Nutritional Value: 260 calories per serving

DIRECTIONS

1. In a large saucepan or Dutch oven, sauté carrots and onion in oil until tender. Add the water, salsa, lentils and salt. Bring to a boil. Reduce heat; cover and simmer for 50-60 minutes or until lentils are tender. Stir in spinach; simmer 5-10 minutes longer or until spinach is wilted.

SOUPS

Butternut Squash and Pear Soup

COOKING: 50 MIN SERVES: 2

INGREDIENTS

- 1 (2 pound) butternut squash
- 3 tablespoons unsalted butter
- 1 onion, diced
- 2 cloves garlic, minced
- 2 teaspoons minced fresh ginger root
- 1 tablespoon curry powder
- 1 teaspoon salt
- 4 cups reduced sodium chicken broth
- 2 firm ripe Bartlett pears, peeled, cored, and cut into 1-inch dice
- 1/2 cup half and half

Nutritional Value: 369 calories per serving

DIRECTIONS

1. Preheat an oven to 375 degrees F (190 degrees C). Line a rimmed baking sheet with parchment paper.
2. Cut squash in half lengthwise, discard seeds and membrane. Place squash halves cut sides down, on the prepared baking sheet.
3. Roast in preheated oven until very soft, about 45 minutes. Scoop the pulp from the peel, and reserve.
4. Melt butter in a large soup pot over medium heat. Stir in the onion, garlic, ginger, curry powder, and salt. Cook and stir until the onion is soft, about 10 minutes. Pour the chicken broth into the pot and bring to a boil. Stir in the pears and the reserved squash, and simmer until the pears are very soft, about 30 minutes.
5. Pour the soup into a blender, filling the pitcher no more than halfway full. Hold down the lid of the blender with a folded kitchen towel, and carefully start the blender. Puree in batches until smooth. Return the soup to the pot, stir in the half and half, and reheat

SOUPS

Mediterranean Soup with Vegetables

COOKING: 50 MIN

SERVES: 2

INGREDIENTS

- 2 tablespoons olive oil, divided
- 1 cup chopped red onion
- 2 cups coarsely chopped green pepper
- 2 large garlic cloves, crushed
- 1 cup sliced mushrooms
- 1 small eggplant, unpeeled, slice in 1- to 2-inch chunks
- 1 (28 ounce) can crushed tomatoes
- 1/2 cup kalamata olives, pitted and sliced
- 1 (15 ounce) can chickpeas, drained and rinsed
- 1 tablespoon chopped fresh rosemary
- 1 cup coarsely chopped parsley

Nutritional Value: 312 calories per serving

DIRECTIONS

1. In a large skillet, heat 1 Tb. oil. Sauté onion and pepper until soft, about 10 minutes. Add 1 Tb. oil, garlic, mushrooms and eggplant. Simmer, stirring occasionally, until eggplant is softened but not mushy, about 15 minutes. Add tomatoes, olives, chickpeas and rosemary. Simmer until heated through, about 10 minutes. Stir in parsley. Sprinkle feta cheese over stew if desired.

SOUPS

Asparagus Soup with Cheese

COOKING: 50 MIN SERVES: 2

INGREDIENTS

2 cups water, divided
1 teaspoon chicken bouillon granules
1/4 teaspoon seasoned salt
1/4 teaspoon lemon-pepper seasoning
1/4 teaspoon white pepper
3/4-pound fresh asparagus spears, trimmed
4 slices process American cheese, diced
1 bacon strip, cooked and crumbled

Nutritional Value: 321 calories per serving

DIRECTIONS

1. In a small skillet, combine 1 cup water, bouillon, seasoned salt, lemon-pepper and white pepper. Add asparagus. Bring to a boil. Reduce heat; cover and simmer for 8-10 minutes or until asparagus is tender. Remove asparagus; cool slightly.

2. Cut off several asparagus tips and set aside. Cut remaining asparagus into larger pieces. Place asparagus pieces and cooking liquid in a blender or food processor; cover and process until smooth. In a saucepan, combine asparagus mixture and remaining water; heat through. Reduce heat; stir in cheese just until melted. Garnish with bacon bits and reserved asparagus tips.

SOUPS

Apple Soup

COOKING: 50 MIN

SERVES: 2

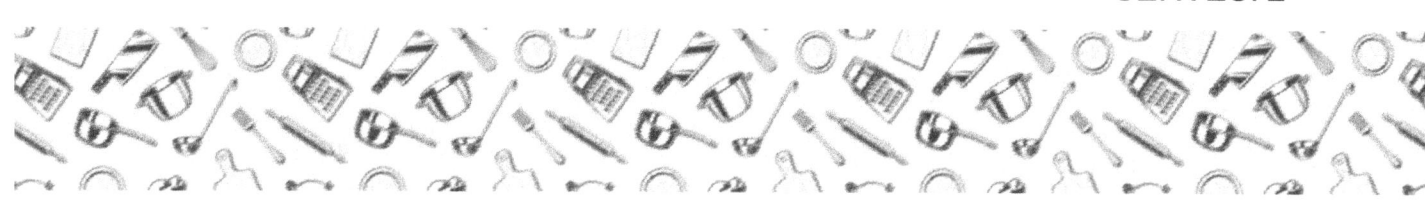

INGREDIENTS

1 lb. apples
1 qt. water
1-tablespoon sago

Nutritional Value: 299 calories per serving

DIRECTIONS

1. Wash the apples and slice into quarters, but do not peel or core.
2. Put into a saucepan with the water and sugar and flavoring to taste. When sweet, ripe apples can be obtained, people with natural tastes will prefer no addition of any kind. Otherwise, a little cinnamon, cloves, or the yellow part of lemon rind may be added.
3. Stew until the apples are soft.
4. Strain through a sieve, rubbing the apple pulp through, but leaving cores, etc., behind.
5. Wash the sago, add to the strained soup, and boil gently for 1 hour. Stir now and then, as the sago is apt to stick to the pan.

SOUPS

Potato Soup with Bacon

COOKING: 50 MIN   SERVES: 2

INGREDIENTS

3 slices Bob Evans® Bacon, slice into 1/2-inch pieces
small leek, white part only, diced
1 (20 ounce) package potatoes
(14 ounce) cans chicken broth
2 cups whole milk
1 cup frozen corn, thawed
1 teaspoon parsley flakes

Nutritional Value: 201 calories per serving

DIRECTIONS

1. In large saucepan over medium heat, cook bacon until crisp. Remove and set aside. In bacon drippings, sauté leeks until softened, about 3 minutes.

2. Add potatoes and chicken broth. Cover and bring to boil, reduce heat and simmer until potatoes are tender, about 15 minutes.

3. Lightly mash with a potato masher. Add milk, corn, parsley and reserved bacon. Heat until hot, about 5 minutes. Refrigerate leftovers.

SOUPS

Pesto Chicken Pasta Salad

COOKING: 20 MIN

SERVES: 2

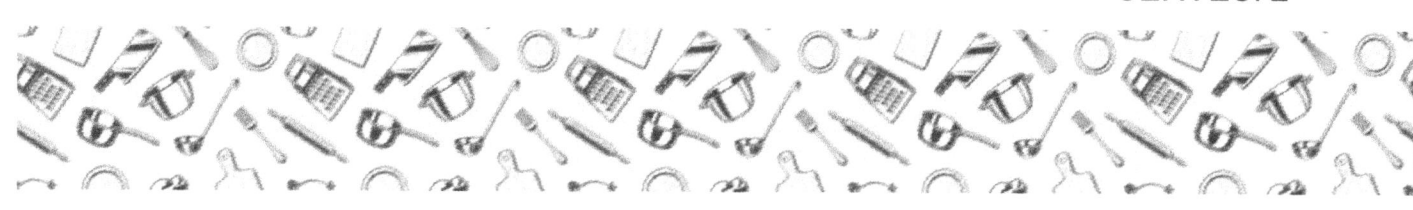

INGREDIENTS

Creamy Buttermilk Dressing:
1 large garlic clove, minced
1/3 cup mayonnaise
1/3 cup sour cream
1/3 cup buttermilk
3 tablespoons rice wine vinegar

Pasta Salad:
2 tablespoons salt
1-pound bow tie (farfalle) pasta
8 ounces trimmed asparagus, cut into 1-inch lengths
1-pound cooked chicken breast strips, pulled into bite-size pieces
8 ounces cherry tomatoes, halved and lightly salted
1 (14 ounce) can whole artichoke hearts, drained, cut into sixths
3 green onions, thinly sliced
1/2 cup pine nuts, toasted in a small skillet over low heat until golden
1/4 cup pesto (homemade or refrigerated prepared variety)

Nutritional Value: 250 calories per serving

DIRECTIONS

1. Mix dressing Ingredients in a small bowl; keep chilled until ready to toss with salad. (Store in clean jar with lid.)
2. Bring 1 gallon of water and 2 Tbs. of salt to boil in a large soup kettle. Add pasta and, using package times as a guide, boil, stirring frequently and adding asparagus the last 1 minute, until just tender. Drain thoroughly (do not rinse) and dump onto a large, lipped cookie sheet. Set aside to cool while preparing remaining salad Ingredients.
3. Place all salad Ingredients (except buttermilk dressing) in a large bowl or transfer to a gallon-size zippered bag. (Can be covered and refrigerated several hours at this point.) When ready to serve, add dressing; toss to coat and serve.

www.ingramcontent.com/pod-product-compliance
Lightning Source LLC
Chambersburg PA
CBHW081355080526
44588CB00016B/2503